UNDERSTANDING WOMEN

UNDERSTANDING
WOMEN

A BOOK FOR MEN

JAN SILVIOUS

PYRANEE
BOOKS

Zondervan Publishing House
Grand Rapids, Michigan

Understanding Women
Copyright © 1989 by Jan Silvious

Pyranee Books
are published by
Zondervan Publishing House
1415 Lake Dr., S.E.
Grand Rapids, MI 49506

Library of Congress Cataloging-in-Publication Data

Silvious, Jan, 1944–
    Understanding women : a simple, straightforward guide / by Jan
Silvious.
        p.   cm.
    ISBN 0-310-34382-8
    1. Women—Psychology. 2. Men—Attitudes. I. Title.
HQ1206.S53   1989   88–13808
155.6'33—dc19   CIP

THE STORIES IN THIS BOOK ARE TRUE. THE NAMES HAVE BEEN
CHANGED EXCEPT FOR REFERENCES TO THE AUTHOR.

Edited and designed by Nia Jones

Printed in the United States of America

89   90   91   92   93   94   95 / LP / 10   9   8   7   6   5   4   3   2   1

To Mom and Dad:
With gratitude for your unconditional love
and the ways you have let me know
that being a woman is special.

To Charlie, David, Jonathan, and Aaron:
Thank you for loving me enough to try to understand.

"From the Author"

"The Great Question . . . which I have not been able to answer, despite my thirty years of research into the feminine soul is, 'What does a woman want?'" (Quoted in Charles Rolo, *Psychiatry in American Life*, 1963).

I believe this brief guide has answers thirty years of research could never yield. It has been born out of my own personal experience of seeking to be understood by the men in *my* life. However, an even greater source than my own experience has been the unnumbered conversations I've had with women over the past twenty years. They have *said* it in many different ways, but the *thought* has always been the same. "I wish the men in my life understood me."

I pray this book will help the men who really want to know what a woman wants . . . and the women who are blessed to have such men in their lives.

Jan Silvious

Contents

"WHY CAN'T A WOMAN BE MORE LIKE A MAN?"   15

ATTITUDE: HOW YOU THINK   21

ACTIONS: HOW YOU ACT   33

AGGRAVATIONS AND ARGUMENTS: 39
    HOW YOU COMMUNICATE

ATTENTION AND APPRECIATION: 47
    HOW YOU LOVE

ASSURANCES: HOW YOU KEEP LOVING   61

"WHY CAN'T A WOMAN BE LIKE ME?"   69

An Unfaithful Wife to her Husband
by Ella Wheeler Wilcox

Branded and blackened by my own misdeeds
I stand before you; not as one who pleads
For mercy or forgiveness, but as one,
After a wrong is done,
Who seeks the why and wherefore.
                                    Go with me.

Back to those early years of love, and see
Just where our paths diverged. You must recall
Your wild pursuit of me, outstripping all
Competitors and rivals, till at last
You bound me sure and fast
With vow and ring.
I was the central thing
In all the Universe for you just then.
Just then for me, there were no other men.
I cared
Only for tasks and pleasures that you shared.
Such happy, happy days. You wearied first.
I will not say you wearied, but a thirst
For conquest and achievement in man's realm
Left love's barque with no pilot at the helm.
The money madness, and the keen desire
To outstrip others, set your heart on fire.
Into the growing conflagration went
Romance and sentiment.
Abroad you were a man of parts and power—
Your double dower
Of brawn and brains gave you a leader's place;
At home you were dull, tired, and commonplace.
You housed me, fed me, clothed me; you were kind;

But oh, so blind, so blind.
You could not, would not, see my woman's need
Of small attentions; and you gave no heed
When I complained of loneliness; you said
"A man must think about his daily bread
And not waste time in empty social life—
He leaves that sort of duty to his wife.
And pays her bills, and lets her have her way,
And feels she should be satisfied."
                                        Each day.

Our lives that had been one life at the start,
Farther and farther seemed to drift apart.
Dead was the old romance of man and maid.
Your talk was all of politics or trade.
Your work, your club, the mad pursuit of gold
Absorbed your thoughts. Your duty kiss fell cold
Upon my lips. Life lost its zest, its thrill.
                                        Until. . . .

One fateful day when earth seemed very dull
It suddenly grew bright and beautiful.
I spoke a little, and he listened much;
A note of comradeship in his low tone.
I felt no more alone.
There was a kindly interest in his air;
He spoke about the way I dressed my hair.
And praised the gown I wore.
It seemed a thousand, thousand years and more
Since I had been so noticed. Had mine ear
Been used to compliments year after year,
If I had heard you speak
As this man spoke, I would not have been so weak.
The innocent beginning
Of all my sinning
Was just the woman's craving to be brought
Into the inner shrine of some man's thought.
You held me there, as sweetheart and as bride;
And then as wife, you left me far outside.
So far, so far, you could not hear me call;

You might, you should, have saved me from my fall.
I was not bad, just lonely, that was all.

A man should offer something to replace
The sweet adventure of the lover's chase
Which ends with marriage. Love's neglected laws
Pave pathways for the "Statutory Cause."

.

"WHY CAN'T A WOMAN BE MORE LIKE A MAN?"

A s he began to speak about his marriage, Larry's face was drawn and serious, riddled with confusion and concern.

"I just can't figure out why she's not happy. I've done everything I know to do to be a good husband. I make good money, so she has almost everything she wants, plus she has money from her own job. I do love her, but she acts like I don't even like her. She says there's something missing and that I never talk to her, but I do! She says that we never spend any time together, but I'm home almost every night! What does she want from me anyhow?"

Larry's thoughts could be echoed by millions of men. Trying to figure out women is a common frustration! Henry Higgins said it so well in "My Fair Lady," "Why can't a woman be more like a man? Why can't a woman be more like me?!"

Can you identify with that statement? Do you sometimes feel that way about the women in your life—your mother or sister, your wife or daughter, your girlfriend, boss, or employee? Do you sometimes think that you must be dealing with a creature whose complexity is beyond comprehension? Does it seem that the task of understanding is too overwhelming and the payoff too small to make the effort worthwhile?

Perhaps you can identify with Henry Higgins' frustrated outburst. You may even remember hearing yourself say, "Women are impossible to understand." I've probably heard that statement in various forms as much as any woman alive. You see, I live in a house with four men—one is my husband; the other three, our teenage sons. At one time or another, each of them has told me how impossible it is to understand women. Perhaps, I have said something that seemed perfectly logical to me but made no sense to my husband. Or, a girlfriend's unexpected response has puzzled one of my sons. Or, even an unknown female driver can convince all of them that it is impossible to second-guess a woman!

Trying to understand why we women do what we do or why we feel like we feel seems to stymie the most intelligent and otherwise perceptive male.

In the last century, John Stuart Mill wrote, "It is only a man here and there who has any tolerable knowledge of the character even of the women of his own family."

In the fourth century before Christ, Aristophanes wrote, "These impossible women! How they do get around us! The poet was right; can't live with them, or without them!"

And yet, if you are reading this book, then you haven't given up! You obviously want to come to a better understanding of and a deeper appreciation for the women in your life. As a woman, I admire that. It takes courage to read something that might challenge your views. I can guarantee your efforts will go a long way toward bridging the gap that so often exists in male-female relationships. So, please read on! I will explain life from a woman's point of view—a view you might find perplexing or even irritating, but a view that is realistic. Although Henry Higgins' question "Why is thinking something women never do?" may have occurred to you,

I will try my best to communicate to you in a way that is logical and practical as we cover five major arenas of life: attitude; actions; aggravations and arguments; attention and appreciation; and assurance.

ATTITUDE:
HOW YOU THINK

*A*ttitudes color every relationship. Attitude is perspective; it's outlook; it's the pink in "rose-colored glasses"; it's the yellow in "a jaundiced view." Every action is influenced by attitude. God says that whatever you think in your heart makes you what you are (Prov. 23:7 KJV). I know that if I think tender thoughts toward my husband, then I will act in a tender way. If I mentally pick him apart, then no matter what he does, he can't win with me. That's the effect of attitude!

Attitudes can be formed before you are aware of them. Years of living with a parent who is negative can leave you marked with a negative attitude that you don't even know you have until you are confronted with circumstances and relationships that tap your prejudice. Think about how the older men in your life have affected your attitudes toward work, toward politics, toward money, and, yes, even toward women!

But, in spite of previous influences, probably you also have within you a desire to get along as best you can with the women in your life, as long as you can maintain your masculinity. (And we want you to hold on to your maleness.)

The essence of the attitude a woman needs is found in four essential words: love, respect, understanding, and acceptance.

23

Love

In the first century, the apostle Paul wrote, "Husbands, love your wives and be not bitter against them" (Col. 3:19 KJV).

In the same century, the apostle Peter wrote,

> "In the same way you married men should live considerately with (your wives), with an intelligent recognition (of the marriage relation), honoring the woman as (physically) the weaker, but (realizing that you) are joint heirs of the grace (God's unmerited favor) of life, in order that your prayers may not be hindered *and* cut off.— Otherwise, you cannot pray effectively" (1 Peter 3:7 AMPLIFIED).

Simply stated, women were given a place of honor in the Scriptures. And the men who married them were told to learn to understand them and respect their position. For the man who would make that effort, there was a bonus: His prayers would not be hindered!

The Scriptures tell the husband that he is to love his wife with the same kind of sacrificial love Christ had for the church. "Husbands, love your wives, just as Christ loved the church and gave himself up for her. . ." (Eph. 5:25 NIV). In plain terms, your love needs to be based on the precious quality of your wife's inner person. It is a love that will give even when there is nothing particularly lovely. It is a love that never considers body build, beauty, or brain. It is based on the simple fact that you *love*. For the man who follows these guidelines, once again there is a bonus: A woman who is loved and knows it is a woman who is responsive to her husband!

To love the way the Scriptures describe is a choice, a matter of your will, because the truth is that we women are not always lovable. But when we are the least lovable, we need your love the most. We need to know that even though you are not receiving what you need at that moment, you are still devoted enough to love us and that you're not considering how you might find love elsewhere.

You may think you are pouring yourself out for nothing, but the natural tendency of women to be "responders" will reward your efforts in the long run. Although it seems as if our modern American society has created a race of female initiators, if a man will love unconditionally, his wife's response will be unbelievably positive in most cases.

Respect

Respect is a term usually reserved for the way we act toward the elderly, the elite, the elegant. However, respect is an essential ingredient for every relationship. It is especially important in the interaction between men and women, between husbands and wives.

Respect is a sense of honor, of esteem. You will give care, consideration, and courtesy to a person who has your respect. And for women, respect can sometimes be difficult to win because of the attitudes that some men— co-workers, pastors, brothers, fathers or husbands—unknowingly have toward women. No matter what a woman does that is noteworthy or creative because she is female, it seems very difficult for some men to acknowledge that she is worthy of honor or esteem.

When my son was born, I remember standing at the nursery window with a young soldier who was looking into a bassinet that contained his beautiful newborn daughter. I commented on her striking beauty. He sighed and said, "Yeah, but every man wants a son." End of conversation. My heart broke for that little girl. If her dad, who is one of the most important people in a girl's life, did not esteem and honor her, she was starting life with two strikes against her! That young father was probably responding to the learned attitude that it takes a "real man" to father a son. Because he had fathered a girl, he felt he just didn't measure up.

• • •

I am the only child of a man who wanted a son. John Robert was to be the name of the boy my father never had. Instead, he got Janet Kay. His only child was a girl. But I always knew that my dad respected me as a person with potential to be whatever I had the talent and perseverance to become! The fact that I was a female, and at times did some very disappointing things that he may not have understood, never dimmed his respect for me. The esteem and the honor I received from my dad was equal to that of a cherished son. Only in my adult life have I realized what an impact the attitude of my father had on me. Because male approval is so important to females, a father is the first man to fulfill or destroy that deeply ingrained feminine need.

Perhaps you are thinking, "It's one thing to show respect and approval toward a little girl who hasn't shamed herself—or me. But it's quite another thing to show approval for a woman who has been a thorn in my side."

True, some women have destroyed the respect that might have been theirs by the immoral, ungodly, disaster-ous way they have lived their lives. That is not the kind of woman I am talking about, although there is a great deal to be said for the redemptive love and respect of a man in the life of such a woman.

The woman of whom I am speaking is the one who is functioning maturely in her role as a woman. She is fulfilling her responsibilities and trying her very best to do the task she is called to do. So few women in this position are truly respected. Or, perhaps they are respected and the men in their lives just don't really communicate, "You have my respect!"

You may say, "Oh, women get respect. That can't be as big a problem as you think." Believe me, as I have listened to women unburden their hearts, respect is a very tender issue with many.

If you want to build bridges with the females in your life, tell the women you work with, the wife you live with, the mother who raised you, the daughter with whom you have been entrusted that you respect her. You might discover that you can make great strides with her if you will sincerely say, "You know, I really respect you. I think you do a fine job."

Understanding

Women are unique! We are not men. Physically we are governed by cyclical hormones that in many of us cause mood swings, depression, physical discomfort, headaches, cramps, water retention, and nausea. At some point in our lives as adult females, it is probable that most of us will struggle with the weakness of menstrual complications, pregnancy, and menopause.

Yes, we can do much for ourselves to relieve this problem. We can make sure we eat well, get the proper exercise, and are under the care of a competent physician. That is not the answer for everything, however! Even though we go to the doctor, we don't always find an answer for our unexplainable physical symptoms. To most men, that is frustrating. Men need answers. If they can't provide an answer or send us to a doctor who can "fix" us, they would prefer not to hear our complaints. Helplessness in the face of our weakness is intolerable to most men. The fact remains, however, that some conditions will leave us physically or emotionally weakened, then we need our husband's understanding.

"Understanding" doesn't mean that you become the victim of our weakness as it is expressed in bad behavior. It does mean that you try to learn about us. Although you can't fully comprehend how we are being affected, you can try to be sympathetic.

A woman struggling with premenstrual syndrome as well as painful menstruation needs you to comprehend that her energy level is low. She is apt to cry over nothing and feel silly or may snap at you. If you can remember that this is temporary and that it is not a reflection on your masculinity or your "husbanding," then you can relax, love her, and wait a few days for the blustery squall to pass.

If you are associated with women in the work force, you won't know exactly what is affecting your female co-worker who is experiencing such problems. But if she is uncharacteristically emotional or snappy, perhaps you could wait a few days before you deal with any stressful issues. That much understanding might make your life a lot easier.

Pregnancy is another time of extreme physical and emotional stress for a woman. Your understanding and help will make your wife's pregnancy a more pleasant experience. Here are some simple, thoughtful things you can do.

1. Be excited. If she wakens you to feel the baby moving, don't be a grump. That's your baby, too.
2. Don't expect her to keep up with you on walks or

hikes, especially during the last trimester. She's probably a little off balance, and as the baby grows, it will be harder for her to breathe.

3. Don't tease her about her shape. She is already thinking she will always look like a pumpkin. If you make comments—trying to be funny—then she will be convinced that you think she'll always be a pumpkin as well.

4. If you have a toddler who still has to be carried, don't let your wife carry that extra burden. It's hard to respect a man who will let his wife carry two babies for him.

5. Be attentive. This is one of the most precious times of your life. You'll regret it in later years if you were so caught up in the things that held your attention that you missed the full impact of your baby's arrival.

The list could go on and on. But from a woman's point of view, I guess the clearest way to express it is, "Do unto others as you would have them do unto you!" If your body looked like that, what would you want your wife to do for you?

If one day, after twenty or so years of living with the same woman, you begin to feel as if you don't know her, then she may be going through menopause. Sleeplessness, depression, painful intercourse, lack of interest in sex, and emotional outbursts are just a few of the symptoms of menopause. You may find that your normally easygoing wife becomes difficult and unreasonable. And this usually comes at a time when you are experiencing some of your own mid-life struggles, so it may seem too much to bear. This is the time when the careful investment that you both have made in your relationship can be squandered and you could destroy your marriage.

If you see this happening, or you are beginning to see some trouble spots coming, don't be hesitant about seeking help. A good gynecologist (not one who says, "It's just in your head") who will carefully trace the problem is your first line of defense. A competent Christian counselor or a pastor with counseling experience could be helpful as well. Just as you would not hesitate to consult a financial counselor if you were in danger of losing your lifetime investment of money, don't hesitate to seek medical or psychological consultation to protect the lifetime investment you have made in your wife.

Acceptance

Every human being needs to feel acceptable. We need to know that someone somewhere approves of us as persons and accepts us just the way we are. That is one of the basic concepts of marriage. "I accept you just the way you are and I love you . . . for better or for worse."

All too often, a few months into the marriage, the harsh spotlight of reality seems to intensify and a husband gets the strong urge to change some of his mate's irritating habits.

She doesn't keep house the way you want her to.

She can't cook like your mother.

She spends too much money.

She talks too loud.

And even the shape of her nose is now irksome to you.

Unfortunately, the spirits of many women are crushed when their husbands begin to comment on things they can't change.

She can be a better housekeeper.

She can learn to cook.

She can get a budget to live by.

She can even learn to modulate her voice.

But the nose is a different matter. And if you ridicule her about it, she is going to wither. Even the things she can change will change a lot faster if she knows that she has your unconditional acceptance. Most women want to please the men they marry, the men they work for, the men in their families. But if a woman senses you are unwilling to accept her for herself, you will find you eventually will have an angry, rebellious woman on your hands.

The choice is really yours. If there are habits, personality traits, or even physical attributes that you find unpleasant, you can focus on those. And in time you can be sure that you will make an impact on your wife. She will become either exceedingly passive or outrageously aggressive. If she has a strong personality, she will conquer life without your approval and you will become less and less meaningful in her life. This won't be what she desires since she would rather have approval from you. But if it's not there, she will look for it elsewhere. And usually she will succeed in finding it. If she has a weak personality, she will "take it" from you, but her original sweetness will become bitter. She may become introspective and critical. Unless you understand her need for your approval, you may never know why the quiet, sweet girl you married has become a cynical, cold woman.

If you will be gallant enough to focus your attention on the qualities that you like about her, tell her how precious she is to you, you will have won a loyal companion and lover for life. God knows what makes women tick; He made us to be responders to love. If you will give it to us without restraint, not only will your

31

prayers be unhindered but you will be rewarded with a wife who will bring you honor.

Your attitude toward women in general will be reflected in the way you respond to the women in your life. Just as men generally have an abhorrence for bra-burning feminists who are out to demean every man with whom they come into contact, so women have a resistance to men who fail to see women as equal, capable, or valuable. If you are experiencing difficulty with the women in your life, or if you really wonder why a woman can't be like a man, your attitude shows your feelings!

For too long, men have allowed their attitudes to be shaped by their male role models, rather than by the clear guidelines of Scripture. To paraphrase: Husbands, live with your wives in an understanding way. If you learn to understand your wife or the women with whom you interact, you will find that your attitude will be the best thing going in your relationship. As your attitude becomes more positive, you will be amazed at the changes you will begin to see.

ACTIONS: HOW YOU ACT

*S*andra had been married three years. Although embarrassed to have to talk with me, she said she just had to ask someone about what was going on in her marriage.

> When Ron comes home from work, he's irritable and may not speak two civil words to me all evening, but then when we go to bed he wants to have intercourse and he whispers all kinds of sweet and sensual things in my ear. Is there something wrong with me that keeps me from making the transition? I lie there remembering what he said about the burned bread at the dinner table, and the last thing I want to do is to respond to Ron.

She had brought up a good point. Because a woman is a responder, whatever her husband has said during the day has to correspond to his actions at night, or she will be angry and feel used. If you make a habit of expecting sex no matter what your attitude has been during the day, you will eventually reap a harvest of bitterness. Actions must be decorated with words and colored with kindness if you are going to communicate to your wife that she is more than a sex object.

As a man you are goal-oriented. Your goal when you're feeling amorous is to have intercourse. The last thing on your mind is what you might have said at the dinner table. In fact, you probably didn't even notice that your wife seemed a little silent while she was clearing the table.

Your wife, on the other hand, is relationship-oriented. When you were irritable at dinner, she absorbed it, but when she went to bed, your comment was still on her mind. She probably was thinking, "What is wrong with me that makes him so irritable?" When you began to caress her, she probably was resentful because now you wanted her to respond to you with tenderness. Yet, you failed to take her feelings into account earlier.

You may think, "That's ridiculous! She knows I didn't mean anything at the dinner table. Why can't she just let it roll off?" The answer may seem simplistic: Relationships are tremendously important to a woman. Your wife's relationship to you is her primary emotional involvement, so anything that might be wrong in her relationship with you—no matter how insignificant it seems to you—is going to have an effect on her.

You can improve your relationship in the kitchen and in the bedroom if you will make an effort to be consistent in the way that you talk with your wife. Remember, a good relationship with you is one of her greatest desires. She will respond to an ongoing, sincere effort on your part to have a pleasant relationship with her.

On the other side of the coin, wives sometimes like to "pet" their husbands—kissing them, hugging them—actually teasing them, even though they don't realize it. Too often, men assume this is simply an invitation for sexual intercourse. But affection is a way for a woman to say, "I love you." If you assume that she is always being flirtatious and has the ultimate aim of making love and you rebuff her or expect more than she intends, then you will find that she will be less and less affectionate. All she wants to do is to reinforce her love for you in a nonsexual way. Try to be sensitive and return her affection on the same level. You will find that in the long run you will encounter less frustration.

Abuse

Verbal and physical abuse are destroyers. Many times verbal abuse will degenerate into physical abuse. If you have ever laid a hand on any woman with any intention other than love, you have violated the deepest part of her spirit. Trust is destroyed in a moment of temper. And although you might beg, plead, and ask forgiveness, abuse will forever cast a shadow on the trust between you and a woman. How is she to know that you will never hit her again? How is she to relax in your care? Will she ever be confident in the knowledge that, no matter how tense a situation might become, she need not fear physical harm?

Adultery and abuse are equally destructive in a relationship. When you are adulterous or abusive, you have violated the two areas where your wife has given herself to you without reservation.

1. She has given her body to you. When you commit adultery, because you and your wife are one flesh, you drag her into bed with you and the other woman.

2. She trusts you for protection. When you are abusive to her even once, you destroy that part of her that depended on you for protection and safety. You jerk her sense of security right out from under her in one moment of temper.

You may not understand why a woman is so distraught when she discovers her husband has been unfaithful to her. You may wonder why a slap across the face or a push across the room can destroy so much in a woman so quickly. Remember, you're dealing with a relationship. And relationships are supremely important

37

to a woman. When a woman gives herself to a man, she sees herself as being protected. If he has a sexual encounter with another woman, he has violated the vows that secured that relationship. If he hits her, he has violated the vows of that relationship. Anything that tampers with the relationship is destructive to a woman's spirit.

If you are young and just starting out in your marriage, why not make a vow that you will never lay a hand on your wife, except to love her? Just as you vow to keep yourself for her only, add to it that you will never touch her except in love. No matter how tense your disagreements might become, if you have determined beforehand that you will never lay a hand on her in anger, you will be forced into a more mature method of handling your problems.

Help

God made women the physically weaker half of the race. If you want to understand a woman, understand that she needs help doing certain heavy-duty tasks. On occasion I have to remind some of the men in my life that, although I can't lift a heavy box, I do have a brain that functions well and I can figure out where to put the box. Physical weakness is not equal to mental weakness. Nothing makes me more grateful than when my husband pitches in and helps me with a physically tough project without comment. That shows me he understands but doesn't underrate my ability.

Have you grown slack in helping the women in your life? A man who is helpful will find that most women will return that help a hundredfold. We need you and we love it when you help without making us feel handicapped.

AGGRAVATIONS AND ARGUMENTS: HOW YOU COMMUNICATE

I n over twenty-one years of being married, and after having a house full of boys in their teens, I have found there are going to be aggravations and arguments. That's reality. But I have also found life can be much more pleasant if we handle those aggravations and arguments in the right way.

Timing, Tone, and Tenderness are the magic ingredients to getting past these rough spots in life.

Timing

Very few things I've argued about have been worth the effort or the pain. The phrase "What is that in light of eternity?" has been a great standby when my fuse was getting short and a blow-up was inevitable. I've seen, too, that as my husband has grown older and mellowed, he has found fewer and fewer things that are worthy of confrontation. But inevitably, the time comes when you have to deal with difficult matters. Whether at home, in the extended family with in-laws and out-laws, or in the workplace, there will be strained situations, even arguments, that must be dealt with in the most positive way possible.

As in most of life, "Timing is everything." If you need to settle a problem with a woman in your life, try to check the territory before you go blundering in to confront her. Is she in a receptive mood? Is she alone without an

41

audience of children or co-workers? Is she pressed with immediate responsibilities? If you are in doubt about any of these factors, then it's better to wait until the coast has cleared.

You also need to check out your own frame of mind. Do you feel calm or explosive? Do you want to "wring her neck" or find a solution? Are you willing to sit down and talk about the problem or do you want to vent your anger and go on? If your goal is to talk calmly and find a solution, then you are ready to talk. Preparation beforehand is always a benefit when you are facing a difficult discussion. You can decide whether you are going to be an instrument of peace or of intimidation.

I used to have a bad habit of failing to enter the amount of checks I had written in our checkbook. This had happened on more than one occasion. Although I knew it irritated my husband and I needed to do better, somehow I just didn't take it as seriously as I should have. Then, the fat hit the fan. We had two checks returned because I had failed to enter the amounts I had written in the checkbook. Not only was it embarrassing, but it cost $30.00. Needless to say, I expected World War III to erupt. I had been asked to cooperate in several encouraging, non-threatening ways.

When I saw Charlie coming, checkbook in hand, I thought, "Oh no, this is it!" Much to my surprise, he said, "Dear (he always says 'dear' when he wants me to listen), your little mistake has just cost us $30.00 and two returned checks at places we do business. Do you think you could put the amount in the checkbook from now on? It would be so helpful." Then he turned and left the room. I was still braced for a tongue lashing, but the timing of his remark changed my habits.

Because he did not approach me in a rage, out of control, I could hear his concern and I wanted to please him. His timing was perfect as were his words, and his gentleness made the difference. How could I dream of letting him down again? And yet, if he had grabbed the checkbook, come at me in a rage in front of the children and called me the "incompetent dolt" that I had truly been, all desire to please him would have been eradicated, and I, too, would have been enraged. No matter how wrong I had been, if he had lacked sensitivity, I would probably still be forgetting to enter the amounts in the checkbook. (If you are wondering why I made that last statement, remember that women are relationship-oriented and men are goal-oriented. Although Charlie's goal was to get me to enter the amounts in the checkbook, the relationship and how it was handled was more important to me. His timing and sensitivity enabled me to achieve his goal and keep the relationship intact.)

• • •

A young man who once worked for me had not learned the importance of timing. He disliked working for a woman but, as the Lord would have it, that's where he found himself. One day, in his zeal to correct me, he dove headlong into a hornets' nest—one I'm sure he never intended to disturb. His timing was so poor that he managed totally to undermine his own point by the way he handled himself. In front of a full staff, he commented in an inflammatory way about all the things he saw that were wrong with me. Not only did he incur my wrath but he lost any support he might have had from any other staff members. He might have had a legitimate complaint, but he destroyed any opportunity to be heard and to be understood because his timing was so poor. Blunt, frontal confrontations may be acceptable among men, (I would question the wisdom of such encounters, even with men) but when dealing with women, I don't think you will reap any benefit by ignoring the circumstances, the surroundings, and the atmosphere to hit the problem head-on. At the least, you will incur anger. And even though a woman may have acquired enough spiritual maturity to take it, you will wound her deeply. Timing is everything!

Tone

Have you ever heard, "It's not what you say, it's the way you say it"? That's what I mean by "tone." Remember, women are relationship-oriented and the way things are said is a part of relationships. If you wrap your words in tones of kindness, you will achieve great things. If you are careless with your tone, then you will reap misunderstanding. Do you find yourself frequently saying, "But I didn't mean that. . . ."? Do you find that you want to communicate one thing but the women around you think you are communicating something else? Then you may have a tone problem!

• • •

I worked with a wonderful man who had no idea that he had the tone of a grizzly bear. Even if he was kidding, this tenderhearted Christian man sounded like he was spitting bullets. I finally learned to interpret what he was saying in spite of his tone, but there were other women who thought he was a boogie man. The truth was, he was a godly man who didn't know how to use the right tone. Other men never had a problem with him; he commanded their respect. I never heard one man ever say anything about his gruff manner, but women who worked with him had to go through the adjustment of learning to listen beyond his tone.

44

• • •

You may pride yourself in being the "drill sergeant" type who gets the job done, but if you really want to communicate with a woman, a kind tone will gain you the respect and cooperation you will never achieve with a bark!

You may be "tone deaf." It could be that you have spoken in a gruff way for so long that you don't even realize you are doing it. Ask the women in your life how you communicate. Ask, "What does my tone say to you?" After they recover from the shock, you'll probably get a straight answer. Just asking them will show that you are not the "old grizz" that your tone might have indicated.

The Scripture says in Proverbs 15:1 that "A gentle answer turns away wrath" (NIV). If you are going to deal with an angry woman, whether she is your wife, daughter, mother, employer or employee, you would be wise to cultivate a gentle tone. You'll be amazed at what a soothing effect it will have in a tense situation, and how you will be admired for being so wise once the air has cleared!

Tenderness

There are two cardinal rules of tenderness: (1) If you ask what is wrong and she says "Nothing," don't walk away. She is really saying, "Please care enough to keep asking. If I see you care, I'll talk." (2) If she is crying, don't leave her alone.

These two rules are hard for you to follow because you are goal-oriented. You want to fix whatever is wrong—that's your goal. If she won't talk or is crying, then you think there isn't much you can do, so you need to move on to other things. When she decides to talk or she gets over her tears, you suppose, perhaps you can get somewhere. For her it is different. She is relationship-oriented, and feelings are important to relationships. If she tells you there is nothing wrong or if she cries or both, she wants to feel that you care enough about that relationship to stay around and do something about it. If you walk off in response to either situation, she interprets that as meaning you don't care!

Whether husband, employer, father, brother, or son, you can help that woman cross her puddle of despair by laying your cloak of attentive understanding across it. You may never realize how important this is, but you will see results in increased communication and, in the long run, cooperation!

Aggravation and arguments are part of every relationship. But handling these irritations with wisdom takes understanding. Understanding does not mean that you are in total agreement. In fact, you may feel that for a woman to be offended by your tone is senseless, but if you can realize that you don't have to agree in order to understand, then you have gained wisdom. If modifying your tone allows an argument to be reduced to a discussion where something can be accomplished, then why not modify? It is a small price to pay for harmony.

Intimidation has never won an argument, it has only delayed it until another day. You may see acquiescence, but you will not see true change until you are willing to be sensitive in timing, to modify your tone, and to be understanding with tenderness.

ATTENTION AND APPRECIATION: HOW YOU LOVE

F or years, I have heard speakers tell women that the key to a man's heart is appreciation. "Find one thing about him that you appreciate and tell him." That's wonderful advice! And it works for both sexes. But I can't remember a time when I've heard men encouraged to give attention and show appreciation to women. Yet with all my heart I believe this double-edged sword could be the death-blow to most problems between men and women. It is tough to continue bad feelings toward someone who constantly expresses appreciation and lavishes attention on you.

There are three places where the kind and quality of attention is important: in private, in public, and in front of the children.

Attention in private is significant to husbands and wives. And yet, after a few years, that private time is usually neglected. Do you ever think about setting aside time to talk to your wife? Or, does she have to wait for the "right" moment to address you? Do you ever plan time alone with her, where just the two of you can enjoy a meal together or perhaps a weekend trip? Do you ever walk by and pat her? Do you tell her she looks nice? Do you express interest in what she wears? If she asks you which dress looks better, will you take the time to observe and give an opinion?

• • •

Some of the first memories I have of my father are captured in permanent photographs filed safely in my mind. He was sensitive to my little girl's need to be noticed and protected. He put Band-Aids on nonexistent sores just because I needed some extra attention.

When I was three, I hated to put on the tight cotton socks that were part of my daily wardrobe. I can still remember in the sleepy darkness of the early mornings when I would feel Daddy putting my socks on my feet before he went to work. Forty years later, it is a sweet memory of security because he saw something that was difficult for me, and every morning until I could manage the chore myself, he did it for me.

There were movies he took me to see, a kitten he bought for me (against his better judgment and my mother's wishes), a pair of stilts we spent one whole day searching toy stores to find, the frequent encouragement of "You can do it," and the ever-present nickname, "Boosie" (for Beautiful Baby). These were the things that built our relationship and let me feel safe with my father.

Anytime Mother or I bought a new dress, Daddy always wanted to see it on us. He made a point to say "Wow!" whenever we dressed for church. Anytime we made an extra effort to look good, he noticed and told us. If there was a style that he felt looked especially nice on us, he said, "You know you always look nice in a long skirt." That holds true to this day!

• • •

I have a theory that daughters who have fathers who admire their clothes and who verbally compliment them will be far less susceptible to men who "come on" to them with flattering words. If a young woman has been fed a sufficient diet of compliments and attention, then she won't crave words of appreciation from just any man who comes her way. She will be equipped to be discerning about the quality of comments and the value of the words she hears.

Listening is very important, too. Even childish chatter that seems to mean nothing is extremely significant to your little girl! If you make an effort to listen respectfully, she will be less likely to look for a "dream boat" who hangs on her every word and then flatters her into bed with him.

Women are responders, and "little women" are responders as well. They need attention, approval, lots of hugs and tender words from the most important man in their lives—YOU. The awkward teen years when your daughter's body is changing, when her complexion goes from peaches-and-cream smoothness to potato-chips-and-coke pimples are years when she continues to need your love and attention. And even if she is not your cuddly, adoring little girl anymore, you are still her daddy and she wants to know you love and respect her. If her dad respects her, loves her, and values her, then she is more likely to respect, love, and value herself in a healthy way.

Maybe your daughter is grown and you feel you have failed her by not being the loving, protective father you should have been. I want to assure you it is never too late! A daughter always wants, and needs, her father's concern, his respect, and his affection. You can begin now to build that relationship, regardless of her age, or yours! The rewards are well worth the effort, and she will appreciate you more than you can imagine!

• • •

Private attention will make a woman feel as if she has your approval. And I've never met a woman who honestly did not care what the men in her life thought of her. In fact, I've heard one statement repeatedly from married women (and I've made this comment myself), "If my husband says I'm okay, then I really don't care what other people think. But if I don't have his approval, attention, and appreciation, then nothing else is right in my world."

In general, men seem to want approval, but it doesn't seem vital to their existence. Women, however, need to know that what they are doing meets your approval. If you doubt that, listen to the ambivalent conversation of women who have been divorced for years. On one hand, they may scorn their "ex" and say, "I don't care what he thinks"; however, on the other hand, there is a deep pain because they could not hold his approval. They always view that part of the marriage failure as their fault even if the husband chose another woman. The little attentions you give her in private are the reinforcements that say "You're okay."

Treatment in Public

A wife is the reflection of her husband. If she is well cared for, it shows; if she is neglected, it shows. How a man treats his wife in public will tell a lot about his character. If he acts as if she is just an appendage, ignoring her at social functions, perhaps even putting her down verbally, then you can be sure he treats her far worse in private. If he makes comments about her weight, her mouth, her brains, then he is announcing to the world, "Yeah, she's my wife, but I don't think much of her."

• • •

I counseled a young couple who were headed for lifelong heartache. I did not know them well, but I had watched their courtship and engagement from a distance and saw a tell-tale sign of death hovering over their relationship. He did not treat her with respect in public. He ignored her and at times made cutting remarks about her. Since I had access to the young woman, I took the opportunity to sit down with her and show her that she was settling for second best if she married this young man.

In her heart of hearts, she knew she was receiving inferior treatment, but she wanted so badly to be married that she was willing to take it. After we talked, however, she made a decision to call off the engagement. We talked with the young man. He left the city and returned several months later, having done some soul-searching. His attitude was totally altered and the relationship resumed. They married and they have had a solid relationship ever since.

• • •

Public treatment is a sign of the true feelings of a man for a woman. The Scripture that says "As a man thinks in his heart, so he is" can easily apply here. If you have negative feelings toward your wife, the women you work with, your mother, your daughter, it's going to show. Or, if you are careless in your treatment of them, it indicates that you are either self-centered or too busy with your own pursuits to give them the proper public attention that they need.

Remember the famous quote "Hell hath no fury like a woman scorned." That is certainly appropriate when a woman is made fun of or derided in public. Remember, we find our self-worth in relationships. If you trespass on our relationships in pursuit of your goals, you may be surprised at the vengeance of our response.

• • •

I attended a lecture by a dear male friend of mine. He was talking about technical things that were not relevant to my area, and yet I was required to attend. I turned to make a comment to a co-worker seated next to me and my instructor said, "Jan, what did I just say?"

I replied, "I don't know."

He chuckled and said, "I didn't think so" and went on with the class.

That little interchange lit a fire of vengeance within me. I felt he had taken advantage of our friendship and had called me on the carpet in front of fifty co-workers. I was enraged; I heard nothing else he said. He had embarrassed me in public. No doubt he had done the same thing to many of his male students who shrugged it off. But as my peer, my friend, and as male to female, he had made an error in judgment. We talked about it later and he said he realized when he saw the expression on my face that he had done the wrong thing. He apologized; I cooled down; and we continued with our mutually respectful relationship. He had the wisdom to know that because I was relationship oriented, I had been hurt by his comment.

• • •

Are you scratching your head again? Or do you understand if you don't reinforce our relationship by your positive public treatment, it can be devastating.

• • •

Sometimes, you will have to sacrifice your own pride even if we don't deserve your positive public treatment. I knew a man who had a wife who could not handle liquor. A few drinks and she was out cold. Whenever he took her to an event where liquor was served, he knew he would either have to deal with her public drunkenness or see that she was taken home because she had passed out. Although their lifestyle wasn't godly and I certainly could not admire it, I was impressed by his behavior toward her. I never saw him treat her with anything but the utmost courtesy. He graciously explained her absence when people asked what had happened to her. And if she was sitting beside him being loud and obnoxious, he treated her with the courtesy he would extend to royalty.

Treatment in Front of Children

A wife has a delicate position to maintain in the home. She is to be submissive to her husband, yet she has an enormous responsibility for her children. If those two pressures come into conflict, then she has a dilemma. The father's verbal support of mother is essential. Even if he disagrees with her mood or method, he should support her in front of the children and deal with her privately about the areas with which he disagrees.

A woman needs to have her children see the respect and the love of her husband demonstrated toward her. If they see the respect, then they will be more obedient because they will understand that they can't play one against the other. If mother says, "This is the way it will be," when Dad comes home, he should say, "This is the way it will be" also. It's hard to manipulate two people who stand united.

When a study of what makes children happy was made several years ago, it was discovered that children wanted their parents to love one another, more than they wanted their parents to love them. In other words, parents loving one another spells security to a child. So loving your wife with tender words, affectionate hugs, and kisses in front of the children is giving them bricks to build their wall of security.

Our boys have always laughed at my husband and me when we have hugged or kissed in front of them. They say "Yuck" but stand there grinning. It's a good thing for the whole family when you express affection for your wife in front of the children.

On the other hand, if you are going to correct your wife, nothing is more demoralizing than to point out her faults in front of the children. If you do it enough, you will probably cause them to choose sides, and if you are the one being critical, chances are they won't choose sides with you. Sometimes, negative comments that started as a little sarcastic teasing can become habitual digs. After a while, the fun goes out and the pain comes in to replace it. If no one is laughing anymore at your house, maybe it's time to stop and look at how you are treating your wife in private, in public, and in front of the children.

If you would like to alter the atmosphere and change the way you are relating to the women in your life, there are three golden words that will help you give attention and express appreciation. They are compliments, communication, and consistency.

Compliments

The Scripture gives a wonderful description of the kinds of wholesome words which are truly complimentary.

> Let no unwholesome word proceed out of your mouth but only such a word as is good for edification according to the need of the moment, that it may give grace to those who hear (Eph. 4:29 NASB).

A compliment should build up. Look for ways you can build up the women in your life. Are they putting in extra effort? Tell them you notice. Do they do extras that make your life easier? Tell them you notice. Is there a flagging spirit in a woman with whom you interact, find something to encourage her with. A wholesome word that builds up costs nothing and will pay off in a woman who feels better about herself.

A compliment should be given when it is needed. A man will endear a woman to himself forever if he lets her know that there is something that he admires about the way she is going through a tough time. If the two-year-old messes in his pants, a kind word of, "You're really doing a good job with potty training," will keep Mom diligently staying after the little guy. A discouraging, unnecessary comment such as, "Can't you do anything with this kid?" takes all of the enthusiasm out of the job. With your off-hand comment that may have meant nothing to you, you have questioned her competence and in the process, you have probably eroded her confidence. She may never say anything in reply, but it is guaranteed that you have just added a brick to a wall that will eventually divide you.

A compliment gives grace to those who hear. If you will compliment a woman in the hearing of others, you have raised her esteem not only in her own eyes but in the eyes of those around her. Compliments about dinner in front of the children set a good example and raise the esteem of their mother in front of them. Compliments about a co-worker raise her sense of worth and will endear her to you for years to come. Because grace is unmerited favor, a compliment given when it is least expected is the most precious compliment of all.

Communication

As much as you can, tell the women in your life what is on your mind. Even though it may seem like trivia to you, because it is of interest to you, it will probably be of

57

interest to her. It is important that you express an interest in the trivial things in her life as well.

Communication is a two-way street. It requires the willingness to talk as well as the willingness to listen. If you want to make a woman feel significant, then talk with her. A poor effort is better than no effort.

It has been said, "Adultery has slain its thousands, silence has slain its tens of thousands." You may not be a talker by nature, but you can be a person who communicates kindness with the few words you speak and by the tenderness of your actions. If you are married, fill her car with gas, clean-up the kitchen occasionally, pat her as you walk by with "I like you" in your touch. Communicate anyway you can, but whatever you do—communicate! Women need it. Don't forget, we are relationship-oriented and communication is important for us to know and understand how the relationship is coming. That's why no woman likes to play guessing games about what you are thinking of her as her employer, as to what you are thinking of her as a daughter, as to what you are thinking of her as a wife. The man who takes pride in saying "I told you I loved you when I married you and if anything changes I'll let you know" is a fool. That demonstrates the greatest ignorance any man can ever display.

Consistency

Many women wish men came with mood barometers attached. Whether they work with men who are moody and irritable or whether they are married to men who are unpredictable, there are many women who have found only one way to cope. They walk on egg shells until they see what his reactions are going to be. Usually wanting to avoid conflict, they will avoid any inflammatory encounters. In some cases that sensitivity is helpful, but when a woman has to suppress her personality because she isn't sure how the men around her will react, problems will inevitably develop.

As a man, pressure and the frustration of your goals influence the way you respond. If you are tired, if you aren't feeling well, or if you just have a lot on your mind, you will find that most women will be understanding, sympathetic, and will give you the room that you need to think and work through whatever is bothering you if you will simply explain. Grumpiness, irritability, silence, moodiness, and withdrawal leave her hurting. Why? Don't forget, we work on relationships. Those are all signs that the relationship is not right and unless she understands that these are things that you are dealing with, she will assume that she is in some way the cause. This took me years to learn. Tiredness makes my quiet, easy-going husband quieter, but at times, irritable. For years, I thought I was doing something that bothered him, but I couldn't figure out what it was. Then I began to do some investigation. Every time he began to act a certain way, he was exhausted, and it would always clear up as soon as he could get proper rest. That kind of understanding really took a load off of my "relationship responsibility." I could act normally, express sympathy for his exhaustion, and relieve as much excess pressure as possible. But more than that, I didn't have to keep wondering what I had done wrong.

If you have women you care about in your life, make an effort to let them know when you are tired or under pressure. You will help them to understand how to relate to you better (which is very important to them) while they help you reach your goals (which is very important to you).

ASSURANCES: HOW YOU KEEP LOVING

T here was a picture in the paper of an old couple who had been married for seventy years. They were both in their nineties but the animation and glow on both of their faces indicated they were delighted to have spent seventy years together. Of course, they had been asked what their secret was. Her response was "love"; his, "I'm not looking for a divorce." In both of those responses there were spoken assurances.

Assurance means that there is a freedom from doubt. Doubt is destructive in any relationship, but for a woman who is very relationship oriented, doubt can be extremely destructive. There are times in a marriage when assurances are particularly needed, when the normal routine has been altered and the woman might be feeling a little insecure about herself anyway.

1. When a woman is pregnant, she needs your assurance that her body is not offensive to you and that you really believe she will be normal again someday.

2. When a woman has gained weight, she needs your assurance that you love her even though it might take her awhile to lose the pounds.

3. When a woman has had surgery, particularly if it has been disfiguring, such as a mastectomy, she desperately needs your reassurance. (By the way, silent acceptance is not reassurance. This is the time for you to muster all the verbal support you can.)

4. When a woman grows older—the late 40s and

early 50s—this may be a time of enormous adjustment. She may see herself changing, with gray hair, a few wrinkles, an extra sag here or there, and she might not be able to see a single thing about you that is breaking down. This could be depressing if you fail to assure her with

"Grow old along with me.

The best is yet to be!"

5. When a woman experiences grief, she needs your assurance that her grief is normal and that she can cry with you. She doesn't have to be strong in your presence and break down later.

6. When the children leave home and the nest is empty, she needs your assurance that you still need her, even if the children have outgrown her parenting. If they have been her total focus, you could lose her to depression unless you really work to say, "Hey, we had each other before they came, and we still have each other now." That's assurance.

There is a special category of women who need your assurance more than any others. If your wife has been the victim of sexual abuse, she will need your assurance, love, patience, and understanding like no other. Women who have been abused have had their trust violated. Abuse is most frequently perpetrated by a man, known to the victim, who is in authority over her. Most often it was someone she was supposed to trust. Then she married you—a man, in authority over her, whom she is supposed to trust. If you know that your wife has this problem, then perhaps some of the following hints will help you assure her.

- Be patient. Although you may not understand it, what has happened to her in the past does have a profound effect on the way she responds to the present.

- Restrain yourself from asking "Why didn't you tell somebody?" That will only add to her feelings of false guilt and condemnation.

- Don't push her sexually. Her response to you will have to come as you build trust.

- Help her seek help. Christian counselors are becoming more knowledgeable and available. In the long run it will help you.

- Control your urge for revenge on her perpetrators. So many women do not share the truth with their husbands because the perpetrator is still alive and in the family. The woman knows that a hot-headed husband could only add heartache to an already unbearable pain by confronting a family member who is a perpetrator. So, concentrate on what you can do to help her, short of seeking revenge.

- Don't be verbally judgmental of her father if he was her perpetrator. Many victims have such ambivalent feelings that include a strong love for their fathers, that any judgmentalism tears them apart. (It may not make sense to you, but remember, you're trying to help your wife get past this situation. If criticizing her father hurts her, then it would be best to leave it alone.)

- Assure her over and over that she has value and that you love her. A victim of sexual abuse has low self-esteem. She usually has to deal with feeling guilty, dirty, unworthy, and useless. If you can find a way to love her securely, then she may be able to emerge from her pit of self-loathing. If you are unwilling to assure her, then you will only push her in deeper. This kind of assurance will require the deepest kind of love on your part, because so often, a woman with low self-esteem will reject your efforts to give her worth. But this is where consistency pays off.

Your character as a man comes through most clearly to a woman when you are going through tough times. You can assure her of your character, trustworthiness, and dependability if you will be willing to

- admit that you are wrong when you are. If your actions have caused her difficulty, you will usually find her ready to forgive if she knows that you will assume responsibility for what you have done.
- admit that you don't have all the answers and tell her you are willing to look beyond yourself for help.

I've known so many women who were willing to seek all kinds of help for their marriages, for their children, for their finances, for their spiritual lives, but with a sigh, inevitably they have said, "But my husband won't consent to go for help."

It all goes back to the fact that a woman will do anything to keep the relationships in her life on an even keel; a man will pursue his goals at any price. For him, stopping to seek another person's help for a problem only slows down the pursuit of his goals, which include, of course, fixing his wife's problem.

I surely don't mean to imply that there are no men who will look for help, but I can say as a rule, it is the woman who will want to look for aid. This syndrome where women know that help is available, and yet, they can't get their husbands to seek help with them, can make women feel very helpless and insecure. She thinks, "This relationship needs help and I can't get the help we need because he won't cooperate."

A man, on the other hand, seems to feel, "It's a phase, it will all blow over, besides I don't know what that other guy would have to say that I don't already know." It's true that the "other guy" might not have anything to offer, but it is very possible that a good counselor could offer insight in a relatively brief time that might prove very helpful. The fact that the husband is willing to seek help gives his wife assurance that all is not hopeless. She also won't feel so helpless if you, as her husband, are willing to try something to correct a faulty relationship. That interest on your part is vital.

Assurance—freedom from doubt—is most easily understood by a woman when she sees a willingness by the men in her life to try to understand her viewpoint and to accept her ideas, maybe not totally, but at least in part. Women are intuitive creatures, and the man who learns to respect that part of her will have enhanced his own life. If you always negate her ideas because she doesn't have a string of facts to back them up, then she will feel that she lacks your confidence. But, if you can listen and give allowance that she just might be right although she is unable to prove why she feels a certain way, then you will have assured her that her opinion is valued. (Watch her intuition. Some women have a remarkable track record, particularly when it comes to smelling a rat long before you spot his twitching nose and beady eyes!)

A wise businessman I know always had his wife meet anyone he was thinking about hiring before he ever offered her the job. He said, "She could sum up that person's character in five minutes. Things it might take me weeks to spot were evident to her immediately." This man, who was eminently successful in business, had the wisdom to listen to what his wife intuitively knew. He quickly admitted how valuable she was to him, and her assurance of her importance to him was guaranteed.

"WHY CAN'T A WOMAN BE LIKE ME?"

I f you didn't know it before, then you surely know it now, that God made women different. Those differences can be wonderfully appealing or horribly appalling, depending on how you choose to react to them. Because women are responders, you will find that any effort on your part will bring a more than corresponding response from her. But, perhaps, you've never known just the right things to do in order to get a positive response. I guarantee if you will apply with undaunted consistency and with undistracted love the principles and concepts outlined in this book, you will make the lives of the women in your life unbelievably rich and you will reap benefits of love and respect far beyond your wildest imagination.

The Scripture asks the question, "Who can find a virtuous woman?" (Prov. 31:10 NASB). And through the years, men have repeated that question in seriousness and in jest, as if to say the search for such a person were futile. Virtue means "goodness" and I believe that a lot of men are working with, married to, and fathering good women. But because you have not understood that most women would gladly respond to your understanding and lavishly return your love, you have treated us, many times, as you would another man, and when we have objected, you have thought we couldn't be understood. But, we can; we need to be; and we want to be women in whom your heart can safely trust.

Jan Silvious is a popular conference speaker. If you would like information about her availability to speak for your organization, write:

Jan Silvious
P.O. Box 23604
Chattanooga, Tennessee 37422